Clouds Before Fire
And
Smoke Before Rain

Winde! Washington-Nnochirionye

COMMUNITY ARTS INK

Printed in the United States for C.A.I. / Waid Books Harrisburg, PA
www.communityartsink.org

ISBN-13: 978-0999470701
ISBN-10: 0999470701

This book is dedicated to my son,

Nkemdilim Taft Nnochirionye
"Nkemo-dilimo-quite-contrimmo-2 named Billy-and the
last one-bimo"
What God has for me, is mine indeed!

For giving me a reason to write.
For finding your Mother's passion cool enough for you to
try your hand at it too.
I look forward to the day that *"Crystal Tears"* will bless my
bookshelf.
Until then, remember, we all cry tears. Some are crystal,
some are ink.
I pray my tears will dry in the form of poetry and stories
and will make a difference in the lives of others,
that they won't have to cry the same tears I've cried.

This book is also dedicated to any one that smells the
smoke and sees the clouds. Don't ignore the warning signs.

They are there. If you can't figure out what you are seeing, write it down. Put it on paper. Write a book. Tell your story. Maybe your fire or your storm will convince someone else to grab a fire extinguisher, an umbrella, or my personal favorite, a pen!

Until pen, paper, and spirit convene again...
I'll be watching the cardinals, keeping my quill moist, and documenting the warning signs.

Winde! Washington-Nnochiriony

ACKNOWLEDGEMENTS

To God, the Giver of every good and perfect gift. To my parents, William Howard Taft Washington Jr. and Randi Massey, for nurturing my creativity and not belittling my imagination. For telling me I could be anything I wanted to be even when I wanted to be a Garbage man. Little did you know then that my song, *"Whatcha Gonna Get From The Garbage Man?"* was the 1st of many songs and poems to come. I was 3 or 4 then. Thank you for acknowledging my imaginary friends and pets. (Though I insist that Bill had the imaginary mouse!) You have consistently supported and encouraged my creativity and imagination. I no longer want to be a "Garbage man". I just want to write about the stuff they get. I do, however, still have imaginary friends. Who knew then that they would be the grown-up characters in my stories today?

To my Big Sisters, Jackie "Jack", Tina "Tin", and my Bae-Bruh, Bill (William Howard Taft Washington III) "Billy-Bill" or "Dollar Bill", for supporting my ideas and celebrating my individuality when the world couldn't understand me. For not making me feel like the "weird kid".

To Grandma, Hazel Ramadan Franks. Thank you, Thank you, Thank you! Every young woman needs a Grandma for a confidant, listening ear, and best friend. I'd like to think I finally recognize the warning signs. Life would be much easier if you were here to point them out.

To my future, Jeremiah 29:11 says, *"For I know the plans I have for you says the Lord,"* We started this journey 7 years ago. If 7 is the number of completion then 8 must mean a new beginning; infinity. Thank you in advance for being a part of what God has planned for us. *"plans to prosper you and not to harm you, plans to give you a future that you hope for."*

To my inner circle, Thank you for listening, for showing up. For clapping and snapping, for previewing, reviewing, and for "liking" my videos and posts. Thank you for being 1-person audiences when I needed to practice and for being publicity managers, photographers, and cheer leaders. Thank you for allowing and at times insisting that I be true to who I am.

I am a Writer. I am a Poet. I am an Author. I am a Speaker.
It's because of each of you that I find courage in writing and speaking about what I see and feel.

Clouds Before Fire And Smoke Before Rain

CONTENTS

Clouds Before Fire
and
Smoke Before Rain

Everything in life comes with a warning sign, she said
And I've spent my life looking for signs
Searching for signs that lead to answers that I can't see
Or questions I sometimes won't speak
I look for signs to point out the obvious
Or at least make the truth, the answers I already know,
palatable
I canvas people's faces
Finding it difficult to trust what I see,
even if it matches what I hear
I still look for a deeper meaning
Connecting words with body language
Finding misleading mixed signals
I can't afford to miss another warning sign
Whispering amen to cardinals in flight
She said, one day she'd be a cardinal
And though I can't be sure it's her
I can't risk that this one may not be the answer to the
silent prayer
An unspoken hope,

her cardinal sign says something good is going to
happen
I pray daily for goodness and mercy
I simply reply amen
A natural sky watcher from birth
I reach for the sky
Somewhere in that vast unreachable space is my limit
My goals and my angels are up there
I watch cloud patterns and admire how God must love
them
How He baptizes them with sunlight and puts them
above the rain
I see what must be majestic presences
I wonder, do they see me?
Big Mamma, both of my fathers, Grandma, my children,
A brother, a best friend, a lover
Do they send me signs?
Do they catalog my questions?
Does Ernest still keep my secrets?
Do they deliberate and confer as a committee for my
fate?
Angels perched on clouds ascending and descending
Am I missing the warning signs?
Surely, I'd be more prepared in life
Instead of standing in fear of the unknown,
Feeling incomplete and void
The signs are so unclear from here

A self-proclaimed meteorologist,
I watch for weather patterns
And whether I chase the storm or the storm chases me
The answer is always in the clouds
And I watch them come and go
Soaking up my tears only to send them back to me,
tenfold
Does anyone see this forest I am in?
Or am I the only one looking at all of these trees?
Am I too close to the problem to see the solution?
Give me a sign
How can you see the fire when it's raining so hard?
My life is a concoction of warning signs, cryptograms,
and mile markers
A story of planted seeds
Indications of growth and life,
Evidence of struggle and sorrow-
Seasons come and gone
Hope for whatever will follow
You'd think by now I would recognize the signs
By now, I should be fluent in sign language
I've been standing in smoke filled relationships
Waiting for the air to clear
Wondering if I'm on fire or is this relationship really
burning down
Rummaging through old baggage and past heartaches
Looking for a clue of what went wrong

Hoping these bags of designer issues I've been carrying
around
Will either catch on fire or at least be the fuel for the fire
I've been waiting for
Asthmatic gasps for air from the density of the smoke
But I can't find fire
Heat from all of life's problems
A burn from the weight of the world on my shoulders
Smoke inhalation and burning are the worst ways to die
And catastrophic ways to live
Burning within from a flame lit from love
Passionate for those things that make life worthwhile
Emotionally combustible,
Dry roots, old relationships, unhealed hurts;
Kindling for even the smallest flicker
I am a forest fire praying for the shade and cover of
whomever lingers in the clouds
Thirsty for the growth of the rain
And how it quenches my curiosities
Cleanses my thoughts,
Washes away my fears, my doubts, and my insecurities
If only the rain could exterminate these fires
If the smoke could dissipate, I could see my own fires
And be a fire fighter instead of a weather woman
If the fire that burns would ignite the good in life
and spread internally from heart to heart
Instead of a community lynching

That same fire would propel us to destinies of greatness
And I'll watch the clouds,
Knowing one day I too will be there
I'll bask in their beauty
Still looking for signs of my loved ones who watch from
afar
Amen-ing at cardinals and roses blooming in off season
Random acts of kindness and butterflies in flight
Will still tickle my spirit and make me smile
Everything in life comes with a warning a sign, she said
There is always smoke before there is fire
And there are always clouds before the rain
Every time I stop to gaze at the clouds
Allowing my focus to shift
Something catches on fire
And when I need the rain to put out the fires
My world is filled with smoke
Is it only my life that has clouds before the fire?
And smoke before the rain?
Or is that another missed warning sign?

CLOUDS

They Areme

(Inspired by 5 different women in the Bible, taken from King James Version of the Holy Bible)

I wonder if my story has already been told.

Has my journey been worthy of paper and pen?

Down through the generations, where would my story
begin?

Could I be so noble to have a history written by those that
came before me?

Etched in time, clandestine, told in signs, and they are
mine because I am them and they are me.

Judges and he judged me not.

He believed in me and he gave me to the world early in life.

Not the warrior and adjudicator of Gilead, but he was a
father and he was my dad.

He walked with authority that wasn't common to the
majority

He fought the good fight like many before.

His life was the wages of his war.

Corporate America and a system that didn't value him was
his battleground.

He was justified. He was dignified.

And then he died and I was the sacrifice.

That day, a part of me died.

I was drowning in grief by the depth of my tears.

I felt alone in the darkness of my unprotected fears.

I covered my soul from the cruelty of life.

I didn't think it could happen again,

but today I see the light.

Ruth, a friend's friend. Helping hands and a tender heart.

I'm loyal to a fault and loyal to my faults.

Walking side by side, wondering how many times will I be

denied? Real love doesn't hurt inside.

Entreat me not to trust thee, entreat me not to love thee

If your sincere friendship isn't worthy of me.

This walk to Bethlehem

This walk with the I am that I am

Isn't about me travelling solo.

It's about Him that I follow and those that I carry

and yes, even those who snare me.

And I'm a little like Orpah, so please don't dare me,

because sometimes I go back to where I came from.

Of friendship and love, I am a humble gleaner;

I just want a Christ-like demeanor.

And still, I fall short of interpersonal behavior

because my template is the Risen Savior,

and no man is an island.

Kindred spirits denotes a kinship, choosing to cherish and

care determines the friendship.

I'll go with you and I'll walk with you.

And I'll carry you and I'll care for you
because I believe in friendship.

Esther- If I perish then I perish.
Who knew that an odd girl that never fit in
Would sit upon the throne and be a natural fit in?
A 20th century Hadassah
I was raised by a league of modern day Mordecai.
And if only you knew my story you'd know the reason why
I try to defy the limitations of external expectations.
I was groomed for success.
And if I've found favor with my heavenly King,
Then my earthly king will offer me up to the half of his
kingdom.
Not his acquisitions or accounts
because in sickness and in health they never amount
And not his shallow words to Vashti-size me,
or to patronize me and parade my naked flaws for all to see
Instead, he'll cherish my inner beauty
and be committed to only me
and the God given duty of his earthly throne and home.
Never forsaking my people
For this I came to the kingdom
For this reason and for this season
And I'll fight the Haman's of society
Addiction, homelessness, illiteracy, and poverty
Though one day, I'll return to the palace

And I still won't escape an ill fortuned fate
if my people are being persecuted.

John – Sometimes I feel like a broken record.
I keep asking the same questions.
And I know this is a test of my faith
Your answers are always yes, no, or wait.
And the fact that You even answer is proof of Your Grace.
She waited 4 days compared to this lifetime
I keep asking questions because You are my only life line.
And yes, I believe so I'll be fine but I gotta ask the question,
"God, why mine?"
I did everything you told me to. I put my trust in only You.
I had lost before but this You knew.
I didn't lose just one child, not counting the others,
I buried two.
Forgive me for my questioning,
If You don't mind, there's one more thing.
Why is it that we pray so hard
And bad things happen in spite of who we are?
Did You know that it would hurt this bad?
I've not done well with disappointment, heartaches, and
losing folk.
You were there when I lost my 2nd Dad.
And I see the lesson and this to my faith I must add.
I've called You because
You're the only choice I've ever had.

I just wonder sometimes if each time You've heard me.

1st John – Her name never mattered.
It only tells you of her status and her stature.
She was a classy kind of lady with a heart full of love.
She demanded that we love one another
as a sister and a brother
And that we honor our elders
like our fathers and our mothers
And when I'm gone and you remember me no more,
just say that God must have really loved her.
He created me. He selected me.
He called me as His own and He elected me.
I've been to hell and back
so it's safe to say, He protected me.
In the midst of my storm
and even when you and I neglected me.
And that's ok because even He was rejected.
See, greater is He that is in me- so He's connected to me
And when things aren't going my way,
He's preparing and projecting me.
And don't be disheartened or confused
I know the adversary objects.
You, see only God knows what's next for me.
And she chose to die rather than denounce her God.
She let go of her wealth and a certainty of health because
loving each other meant more to her.

And it's hard to love unconditionally that way
But I've got a heavy cross to bear that I carry every day.
Only agape love can free your mind,
your body, and your soul.

My stories are told in every language
and on every corner of the earth.
It's what I do with what He gives me
that ultimately determines my worth.
And though my circumstances may differ,
my obstacles seem insurmountable and my successes few.
Please don't pity me, wish you were me, or judge me
because you don't know what I've been through.
Just remember that I am human,
trying to make my way to heaven.
I've unmerited favor by His Mercy
I'm saved by His Grace it's true.
I am a work in progress and I pray that you are too.

*Dedicated to Minister/Sister/Cousin/Aunt Odessa Brown for
escorting me across the desert sands and carrying me when the
sand was too hot.*

*For Daughter Patricia Hollowell for being an example, a warm
smile, and wisdom when the labyrinth was most confusing.*

For Sister Goldie Bishop (posthumously) for being an unlikely ally in unfortunate circumstances. I will never forget your words or your request.

For Past Grand Joint Council President, New York State, Sister Sara Rovena McFadden (posthumously) for showing me the ropes and not letting go when the assignment was complete.

For Past Grand Matron of South Carolina, Mother Bernice Walker. Thank you for choosing and trusting me to serve with you as your Associate Grand Matron. Thank you for your prayers, our daily conversations, your friendship, your Sisterhood and for deeming me "Precious" when I needed it most.

To S.O.U.L. of Adanna #129, Greenville, South Carolina; (truly God's favorite Daughters), thank you for allowing me to share what each of these women have taught me. Thank you for letting me share something I love in the best way I know how. Thank you for SOUL! Thank you for entrusting me with one of the greatest honors a Sister can bestow upon another Sister, Worthy Matron. Thank you for supporting me and, as I always say, for being Aaron's and Hur's when I grew tired and or weak. My prayers are and will always be that I remain Worthy.

To each of these women, thank you for being fine examples of Adah, Ruth, Esther, Martha, and Electa. Truly, that's who you are. And because we are all an extension of each other, I am them because...

Writing the Vision
(Inspired by the Book of Habakkuk)

Like the sweat that poured as blood from his veins
In the garden of Gethsemane,
My visions and my questions turn to words
And run through my veins and out of my fingertips until
poems form
And susceptibility pours onto my page as the best of me.
I have questions
And my questions have questions.
While I know that You are
All seeing,
All knowing,
And You hold all power in your hand
My thinking is limited
And my thoughts can't reach Your thoughts
But I can't help but wonder,
Why? Why the suffering?
There are oceans filled with our tears
And mixed with our blood
You parted that Sea before,
And how?
How can people be so hateful?
How is it that a people created in your image;

Beings built to love and built to be loved
How can we cut each other down like grass left to wither?
And what about our daughters?
What of their virtue?
How long will babies have babies
While our sons don't have fathers to show them the way?
How many of your people will die from depression and no
direction?
While others are snatched from our grip
By low self-esteem, self-loathing, and a lack of love?
When will our men take their rightful places upon their
thrones
In God's original institutions; our families and our homes?
And in exchange for chasing material riches
Like blood diamonds and fool's gold,
When will our women submit to our men?
Not as inferior beings or subjects of their pleasure
But as forces with which to be reckoned;
As the rib, resilient enough to protect the heart
And firm enough to support the backbone.
Our kings and our princes are being hunted like wild game
And our daughters are sought as marketable merchandise.
Bring Back Our Daughters and Black Lives Matter
Are 400-year old campaigns.
In your infinite wisdom, you knew this.
I just need to know if this is the plan.
We are operating in a spirit of fear.

I just need to know!

Does our heightened alert status reach on high?

Do my questions warrant answers?

And yet I see Your Glory.

I see Your miracles daily.

I would be remiss if I didn't wonder,

Have I strayed too far from you?

I know that You reject and rebuke the filth and squalor that
we've created.

I just have to know, what happened to our story?

What price did we get for our pride?

Can a freedom that you paid the ultimate price for be
pawned and re-redeemed?

How did we lose its value?

Have we wagered our birthright?

Can your manna not fall from heaven for us again?

We are becoming a people so far removed from who we are

Our story is being rewritten by Geppetto

To make us as marionettes

Held by twisted strings and hung by knotted ropes.

How long will we be the fruit that hangs from their trees?

And if I write what I see, will I ever write a love poem?

Will things ever get better?

My pages are filled with emptiness

My people are empty vessels

Filled with empty promises and are void of your vision.

How many poems will I pray from the abundance of my

heart?

And how many prayers will I write?

How many times will I write of things as though they were

real?

I can write the vision but you are the artist.

You provide the scenery and the subject.

Disharmony lends its color to my ink

Confusion and distress intertwine themselves as

parchment for my poems.

I can make it plain.

I can write the brutal truth

Or the truth that I see from the depths of my soul.

My poems are my platform

My words are a podium

Giving meaning to a message beyond my comprehension

From a place of purity that I can only hope to see.

With clarity, I can write your message

A broken people with division amongst them can run in the

same direction

But they will never be whole.

Your vision tarries and we are waiting.

Hope has escaped us and our spirits tire.

I know your Word to be infallible and true.

But between ascension, deceit, hopelessness,

and the trickery of this world,

Waiting on a vision that we can't see is hard for a people

that have been through what we've been through.

I will sit on high and write.

I will speak from my heart.

If you give me the words- I'll write for healing.

I'll use my pen as an instrument of change.

I will write of hope for the hopeless and of abundance for those in need.

You are the true Poet from on High.

Give me your Words to engrave in my heart

and publish to Your people.

I will write.

Draw me near that your vision may be clear to me.

I will write.

Show me the vision and I will transcribe.

Let my pen be dipped in truth that they may see you.

And though your vision may tarry

Let us not be fatigued in our anticipation.

Let my words flow from heart to heart.

If you give me the poem, if you grant me the favor of vision

I will write.

I will sit on high and speak from my heart,

I will make it plain and write the truth.

And though the vision is for an appointed time

and it tarries,

We will wait.

We will labor for it.

We know it will come

And it will not lie..

Hide and Seek My Soul

One, I'm it, run,

Two, three, my soul, I've got to,

Four, find my,

Five, soul.

Where does one,

Six, look for the,

Seven, smile in life?

Eight

Or the spirit that says,

Nine, keep walking?

And ten, what do I do,

Eleven,

Without my soul?

Twelve

Where is my soul?

Thirteen, fourteen, fifteen

Behind the trials, sixteen,

And tribulations, seventeen,

Or under my, eighteen,

Puddles of disappointment?

Nineteen

Too big, twenty,

For my mountain,

Twenty-one, of misfortune.

Too bright for my, twenty-two,

Mole hill of pressure.

My, twenty-three,

My, twenty-four,

My soul.

Twenty-five, where would a soul

Twenty-six, hide?

I need my soul.

Twenty-seven

I need the, twenty-eight,

Determination that makes me,

Twenty-nine, laugh

When others are, thirty, thirty-one

Laughing at me.

I need the, thirty-two,

Will to go on.

And the confidence, thirty-three,

That says, thirty-four,

Eventually,

Thirty-five, everything will be okay.

Thirty-six, my soul keeps running.

Thirty-seven, I want my,

Thirty-eight, secrets.

I want my, thirty-nine, poetry.

I, forty,

Want my self-esteem.

I even, forty-one,

Want the, forty-two,

Mother, forty-three,

That my soul holds back.

My soul, forty-four,

Is hiding in this, forty-five,

Life tunnel.

And, forty-six,

I keep looking.

I think, forty-seven,

This is, forty-eight,

Called, forty-nine,

Soul searching.

Fifty, fifty-one,

All I want is to,

Fifty-two, find my soul.

I'm searching deep.

Fifty-three

In this pool of confusion and,

Fifty-four, blackness.

Beneath, fifty-five,

Pain, and beyond, fifty-six,

These obstacles.

Fifty-seven

My soul.

Fifty-eight, right by peace, love,

Fifty-nine, sixty,

Unity, tranquility,

Sixty-one, sixty-two,

I found it.

Sixty-three

One soul.

twenty-three years old.

And it only took sixty-three tears this time.

From Baby Dolls to a Cardinal With Wings:
Hazel "Grandma" Ramadan-Franks

When mom said I was too young,
You introduced me to Colored Girls Who've Considered
Suicide
The world's shortest giant
You said the rainbow is never enough
My childhood friend in a previous life,
We are kindred spirits
Barren but not childless
Childless but not barren
You can't be defined
The neighborhood watch,
You are encouragement in my dark places
Forgiving but not forgetful
You couldn't be held down
Cigarettes, coffee, and cough drops
Sam Cooke finding respite and sleeping on your couch
You introduced me to Khalil Gibran
Self-Educated, full of Grace
First generation survival of a survivalist mentality
You freed my left hand and uncaged the hiding writer
Smoke before the fire and a cloud before the rain

You taught me to watch for the warning signs
You were my partner in crime and my enabler
A lover and speaker of the Kings English
In the after-life you are a bright red cardinal
Except still female and definitely nocturnal
The original night owl, we stayed on the phone until dawn
Simultaneously and unapologetically Muslim, Catholic,
and Baptist
The wife of a first-generation Greek immigrant
Always prepared, plastic bags in your boots
You crossed racial barriers
You defied parental imposed curfews
You were the solution to every teenage dilemma
A social activist,
My secret keeper
A poet and a writer before your time
A friend when your time was up
This little light of mine, As-salumu alaykum
Thou art blessed

This is for You!

We acknowledge you on this special day
For the care and the love that you gave
For your strength and resolve in uncertain times
Though you were scared, somehow you were brave

This is for you

For the times that I fell and the tears that I cried
You stood me up and wiped my fears away
You were stern, yet yielding, filled with pride and
compassion
You gave me wisdom for life's rainy day

This is for you

When others wouldn't stand by me, you were there all
along
Meeting my intellectual and emotional need
Selflessly, in the gap you have stood and remain tirelessly
standing
It is a thoughtful and often thankless deed

This is for you

Whether Father by birth or Dad by association

Whether paternal or simply man I adore

You're an example, a mentor, a provider, and friend

The likes of which the world could use more

This is for you

For a season or lifetime or through a journey I'll travel

Father- one of life's greatest resources to be had

We may not say it often, we appreciate and love you

So, this poem is for you Dad

Written especially for and dedicated to my Dad, William Howard Taft Washington, Jr. and my Pops, Lonnie Massey, Sr. One who gave life and started my journey and the other who stood in the gap. I love and miss you both!

Day Bass

Yesterday you came home
And the world was at your feet
Your horizons were limitless
And your obstacles few
You came home
And you brought with you an abundance of love
We had never known

Yesterday,
At dawn, you appeared miraculously into our lives
You were exactly what had been missing

It was barely dusk
And you had already learned to walk and talk
You were gracing our lives with your laughter
And wooing our hearts
With your innocence
You made us proud
With your youthful wisdom
And impressed us with your determination

Nighttime had barely reached its' splendor

And you were already crossing the streets alone
You were making your own friends
And testing the waters beyond our protection

Just last night
You were forming your own opinions
And asserting them too
You were coming into your own
And reaching for different horizons

In the wee hours of the morning
You stepped up the tempo
And began walking to your own beat-
Bass

This morning
You started fighting your own battles
When you knew we would fight too
You put on your armor
You went for
And held your own
Because you knew what you wanted
And would accept no less

This morning
You confronted your fears
The best you knew how

And just because you tried
You emerged the victor

This afternoon
You claimed your manhood
Not by age, but by rite of passage

You took whatever life had to offer
You faced it
When fate tempted your favor
You picked up your tuba
And played your own song
But for some reason
Life doesn't always dance to our music

You opened our hearts and walked in

Just yesterday, your demeanor was untainted
Just yesterday, you came home
And already your tomorrow is not promised

Clouds Before Fire And Smoke Before Rain

FIRE

The 31 Word Lie

I pledge allegiance to the flag of the United States of
America and to the republic for which it stands, one nation,
under God, indivisible, with liberty and justice for all.
A 31-word fabrication
written in 1892 by socialist minister, Francis Bellamy
Oh, beautiful for spacious skies,
 I've always wanted to be patriotic,
 I've always wanted that pride swelling experience
when the flags are raised
or carried by
as people place their hands over their hearts
The original flag salute was to extend your hand toward the
flag, palm down
 In WWII, concerned that this salute resembled the Nazi's,
 it was changed to what is used today
But that wasn't all that resembled what the Nazi's did
and so somewhere between raising a hand to a symbol of
misogyny and oppression
And placing my hand over my heart
I raise my fist, tightly clenched, to symbolize a grip
on the truth and an unwillingness to accept the lie
I pledge allegiance to truth and righteousness
In a classroom in anywhere, USA

where the books refuse to tell the truth
 about two-thirds of a population
by omission and a process of elimination,
these students don't hear about the Great Passage
of their ancestors
 and I want to be a proud American like Chevy and apple
pie
but I wasn't included in the Constitution
and though Whitney Houston made it sound good,
verse one is just a cover
 and verse three tells a 40-word truth,
"No refuge could save the hireling and slave from the terror
of flight, or the gloom of the grave.
And the Star-Spangled Banner in triumph doth wave, o'er
the land of the free and the home of the brave."
Why do we only sing verse one
 of a 4-verse national anthem?
O say does such a banner of freedom yet wave?
Those same students in my town, USA are tested
 with an across the line standardized test in the 4th grade
to provide statistics to the Department of Criminal Justice
predicting and anticipating residents for
the belly of the beast before they even reach puberty
But those same numbers don't get books or better schools
So, a high standard test is given in low standard schools
where the administration has a deficit in cultural diversity

and there are underpaid teachers who don't even know the
difference between
the action verb of My Mamma be gone and the definitive
statement of My Daddy is gone
And I want to be patriotic
When my country fights for the freedom of the masses,
I want to say I am included
They swept racism under the rug
and hid discrimination in the shed
where they carefully hid the whites' only signs
They forgot to cancel bigotry and instead gave it a position
with authority, a gun, and a gavel
and now we carry Black Lives Matter signs in a nation
that's supposed to have justice for all
I place my hand over my heart because self-preservation is
survival's first law
In 1893, Katherine Bates petitioned God to,
"Shed His grace on thee"
She continued,
"Till nobler men keep once again,
thy whiter jubilee"
I want to believe that though I was included in the huddled
masses that reached the shores from sea to shining sea, the
great American dream includes even me
Soldiers fighting to the death for an indivisible nation that
intentionally sacrificed their brown skin soldiers to confuse
their darker colored enemies

Our men departed for a purpose and a cause to return as
broken souls
Their bodies mangled and their minds marred
only to find that the dream of returning home as heroes
was replaced with
 a consolation prize of 2nd class citizenship
and their bodies bound with melanoma and disease
We should all have PTSD
And why do so many Viet-Nam vets have colon cancer or
some other form of malignant carcinoma?
Perhaps Miss Ever's boys
weren't America's only human lab rats
I want to say I'm proud to be an American
but America isn't proud to have me
Our fellow compatriots called us refugees in Katrina
And FEMA or the Federal Encouragement of Missions or
Matters Abroad
thought that a two-thousand-dollar gift card and a metal
shipping container as a home
could replace the losses of an entire region
while they stood by as we watched our families being torn
apart for the umpteenth time in American history
The levies of equality have been compromised, breached,
and are broken
And I'll snap for myself because I know I'm telling the
truth

I want to be patriotic instead of an orphan bereft of a
nationality
I came as a slave then a Negro, colored, black, an afro, and
African American
Only two countries in the world characterize their citizens
by the color of their skin
One can now boast an end to apartheid
and America won't even admit that apartheid would be the
sniffles
compared to the racism and partial hate that has plagued
her land
America has bastardized a whole race of people
who have built this sweet land of liberty with their bare
hands
and have sacrificed life and limb just to be accepted or at
least not excluded
The lie speaks for itself
and the truth, well the truth will set this country free
You can't be under God until you are truly indivisible
and it's not liberty or justice if it's not for all
America, just mean what you say or say what you mean
Until then, I'll be watching your every move,
questioning your every proclamation
and pointing out your deceptions and misrepresentations,
holding up my fist as a sign of my allegiance to what's fair
and right
and my refusal to accept anything less

And, America, until you get it right,
I'll just be a proud Americanized-African

This is an account of a true story, told in Pidgin.
A Native Story in a Native Dialect

I saw him.

I saw him in the heat.

Not just heat but the hellacious heat of the Lagos sun on
Oshodi Road.

Between Apapa to Ibadan coming from Festac to the third
mainland bridge.

Conductors weaving through cars on mobile morgues-

Vans turned into buses,

Doors removed to accommodate additional passengers,

Victims as we call them in my village.

Traffic for as far as the eye can see.

We no get traffic lights and stop signs.

This one is every man for self, shah.

See, I may be new to this land,

But I no be JJC. I no be Johnny Just Come.

I am a native to this village.

They say I be Oigbo- White, because am American.

Yoruba have even called me Tokunbo-

Like saying I have returned

There was this man.

He was just there.

Not just standing there, you understand?

Ah ahh! This one, he was dead.

The driver-whey see him first says, "Auntie, look away."

I can't. I no fit look away.

My eyes fix in his direction.

Now me-o, I've neva seen a dead man.

I have seen a man that has passed away-

But this man was lying on the street, dead.

His body dey dusty.

He was covered in the hot dry Nigerian dust

Like Earth to Earth.

And the cars- ha- the cars, they just keep going.

And de people (sucks teeth) they keep moving too.

Ah ahh! How come now?

The driver makes the sign of the cross.

I can only say, in my native, native tongue, "Oh my God!"

Forgetting that my main goal is to be less of me and more of them.

In Pidgin English, I translate, "My God!"

I try Igbo on for size, "Cineke!"

And I dash in a little more pidgin, my new native tongue.

"God's pikeen no fit find honor -o."

God's children will never find honor.

My eyes go back to the man- the dead man, shah.

I don't' know him.

This one I no sabe.

I know he is our brother.

He is a son, a friend, maybe a husband or a father.

You understand?

Ah-ahh. Driver, I say, "What kind of thing is this?"

"See, eh, in my village, you can't just leave him there."

"You must take him to the hospital."

"No Auntie, ah beg, I no go 'gree." He says

"Now, this wahalla no be ours today."

I say to him,

"In my village-eh, wahalla/ trouble be just that; trouble."

"And if my brother or sister get wahalla, then I get wahalla self."

The driver no fit listen- he won't listen.

Een no go gree. He won't agree.

The next day, riding down Oshodi Road to Ikoyi Island,

They are all there.

Women in bright colors with wrappas and lace and Jesus of Nazareth Sandals

Walking in Jesus of Nazareth dust and heat.

Some dressed for work.

Children in school uniforms.

They move robotically and methodically to an unheard rhythm that you can only see. Babies on backs

Children chasing closely behind women with their fare on platters balanced on their heads.

"Pure Water!" Pure water! The women yell.

A child says, "Auntie, make I bring you oranges"

And makes a sign to beg for money.

I buy the water packaged in sandwich sized plastic bags.

I know it's not pure and I'm not sure it's water-

Am certain this is on the CDC list of things NOT to

consume.

But I am home.

I am as Nigerian as they come.

I am Nkechinyere, a gift God has given.

Gapped teeth, coarse hair and a village in my heart and my

heart in my village.

I buy the oranges in the bag and a roasted ear of corn with

the roasted coconut.

Na me-o, I don't even like coconut self.

But the scent of the corn and the fruit,

and the earth, and what must be God

has me mesmerized, hypnotized, captivated and awestruck.

I say, "Driver, I no fit be late for work shah,

I go wakka faster than this car. I beg, drive now."

We drive and the driver says, "Auntie, Wale window. Close

the window!"

I wale, I wale, I close the window.

He is Yoruba- from his language and his tribal marks.

He is beautiful but aromatically incorrect.

I no fit wale window but shah, I no get time for wahalla this

morning.

And then I see him,

I see am and he is even dustier,

and no less dead than he was yesterday.

I forget my new language and I cry for him in de sweetest

language I know,

"Jesus" I mean, "Cineke."

I fit tire for this language barrier-o.

The driver also translates,

"Baba. Baba-o",

I hear him say in Yuroba.

On the third day, I dey search for am, shah.

The man, he is gone-o.

His body no longer adorns the dusty Oshodi Street.

Men and women continue to vend their wares.

The conductors standing on the vans slash buses whey the

door dey removed,

Yell street names and transfer points like a song or a chant;

Badagry, Oju Elegba, Ikorodu, Ikeja, Surulere!

 The street is so packed, you no sabe if you fit move or you

dey stand still.

You understand?

People dey move with traffic like cars.

Cars dey roll by like people.

Today, shah, I no fit chop oranges or drink pure water.

I beg, make me see suya and moin-moin,

And the little girl with the pretty teeth that begs for money.

Today, shah, make am bring sweet fresh mangoes,

Whey de juice dey run down arm-o.
Today, just one more day, I no fit see "Uncle",
The name I go call the dead brother when he comes to
mind.

How come? I ask myself.
How I go be big boss or "Oga" with a driver and security?
And how I dey do Madame with big gele tied on my head
But I no see fit for save de people-o?
When I dey see man where lay for street dead,
I dey see him in my village tongue.
English no get words for this one.
America no fit allow such things.
You see eh? This one na lie down for street and then die.
Here, in America,
We go die first and then wakka from place to place.
Same reaction-o!
The cars go drive by-o!
And de people, dey fit cover face and cross street-o!
The stench of life sometimes be just like the stench of
death.
Wale window be like wale eyes, wale mind, wale ears, wale
heart.
Close them all.
Auntie, look away.
I no get time for this kind of wahalla!
In America, we go say, "Ain't nobody got time for that!"

How come-o? Since when we go let man die for road?

What happened in this village where we no see fit for save man, eh?

I beg, make I go sit with village elders.

I go gist with dem and yan with dem.

Sit at their feet and sip knowledge or the purest water.

We go break and chop sweet agege bread.

We go chop suya and fried plantains or edodo

While auntie makes pounded yam and foo foo.

We go drink palm wine from the drinking gourd.

I go ask them what happened. Where we dey go wrong?

Whatin we dey do-o? What have we done?

I no sabe the day where I go forget Uncle lying dead on Oshodi Road.

I dey see am now.

I go remember uncle in my prayers always.

In my village, I go always tell this story. This Akoko.

I fit say it in the language where I dey saw it.

I go tell a native story in a native tongue.

Maybe his story go bring back life on another road and for a different dead situation-o. *(Maybe his story will bring back life on another road and for a different dead situation.)*

One day, shah, I pray I go see Uncle in eternal life.

I go greet am.

This time, I go be JJC; Johnny just come, you understand?

And I no sabe if God dey speak pidgin.

I don't know if God speaks pidgin.

But in my village, I go wait to hear God say,

"My pikeen, my child, you dey do well well-oh. You have done well"

I go think in my native-native tongue, "It wasn't easy", you understand?

But I go say, "Life-eh?"

"Now this one no be small thing- shah."

Glossary

*Pidgin (pĭd-gĭn) English infused with many Native African languages. This language has been incorrectly referred to as "broken English". Other forms of languages and cultures infused with indigenous African languages include, Gullah, Geechie, Creole, and Patois.

Ah beg (Ah bĕg) I beg. To plead or ask please. Literally, I beg of you.

Akoko (ah-kō-kō) A story

Am (ahm) Them, him, her "I see am" (I see him), also used instead of I am.

Baba (bah-bah) Yoruba word or father or God

CDC – Center for Disease Control

Chop (chop) To eat

Cineke (chēē-nay-kay) God (Igbo word)

De (dĕ) the

Dey (dāy) various tenses of the verb to be, is, was. *How body dey?* How are you feeling. A common, comical response would be: *Na body dey inside clothes.*

Fit (fit) Want or willing to.

Gelé (gāy-lāy) Head wrap made of hardened damask. The material feels and sounds like paper. It is stiff and allows the head wrap to be shaped and arranged. Particularly higher than a head wrap made of fabric.

Get or **No Get** (gĕt) To have. *I no get money. I don't have money.*

Gist (jĭst) Talk or converse, dialog

Gree (Grēē) To agree. *No go gree* is to disagree

Igbo (ēē-bō) A tribe and language from the western part of Nigeria

JJC – Johnny Just Come, someone who has just arrived, usually a foreigner. I no be JJC is like saying, "I'm not new to this game."

Madame (mah-dahm) Madam, a lady, or the lady of the house. Generally, an established woman. A term of respect.

Moin-moin (mō-ēēn mō-ēēn) Steamed black eye peas with the black eyes removed (an exercise of patience). The black-eyeless peas are ground with onions and seasoning. The mixture is poured into a foil pocket or empty tin can and steamed until stiff. Different ingredients like canned meat, shrimp, or a boiled egg may be added.

Na (nah) Now

-o (ōh) Usually added at the end of a word to emphasize the word. *This food is fine-o!*

Oga (ōh-gah) Boss

Oigbo (ōh-ēē-bō) Igbo word meaning white person

Pikeen (pee-keen) small child or children

Sabe (sah-bē) To know something

Shah (shah) Dear, honey, a term of endearment

Suya (sū-ē-yah) Meat (usually chicken or goat) on skewer sticks, dipped in oil infused with various seasoning and grilled on an open grill. Served with red onions and red pepper.

Tokunbo (tō-kūn- bō) Yoruba name meaning from across the seas, from overseas

Wahalla (wah-hah-lah) Trouble, problems, issues

Wakka (wah-kah) walk

Wale (wah-lāy) Yoruba word for close

Well-well (well-well) To add emphasis on an adjective, it is simply repeated twice. *You dey speak pidgin well-well-o.*

Whatin (what-tēēn) What thing. *Whatin you dey do? What have you done or what are you doing?*

Whey (wāy) Where or that

Wrappas (rap-ahs) Wrap skirt made of colorful fabric, wrapped and tied around the waist

Yan (yahn) To talk with someone, communicate, dialog

Society's Zoological Garden

Captivity,

A wild specimen taken from the original environment

Estranged

This creature different from the rest

Stuck in a world so new

Withdrawal

Various articles placed nearby to simulate the original

setting

Depression

Trying to fit in

Culture shock

Resisting adaptation

Ethnocentricity

Thinking of what home was like

Nostalgia

Wishing for all the things that were

Oppression

Forced into an unclaimed, unwanted, callous status

Captivity

**WELCOME TO SOCIETY'S ZOOLOGICAL
GARDENS**

Please do not feed the animals intellect

And please do not touch the animal's emotions

"To the left, ladies and gentlemen, you will notice specimen
number one
Homo sapiens, we call it!"

Captivity

Three pens past the polar bears
Sharp left of the mountain goats
Right before you get to the reptile house

Caught
Captivated
And stuck
Scared
Angry
And confused
Nevertheless,
Captivity

"WE DO HOPE YOU ENJOY YOUR VISIT AT THE
BEAUTIFUL AND PLENTIFUL
ZOOLOGICAL GARDENS OF SOCIETY"

Deadbetedness

There is a plague that has infiltrated our communities
I'm convinced that its statistics are more horrific than
AIDS,
more debilitating than any addiction,
this malady is traumatizing and tormenting our people
My people
My family
My child
This sickness is painful; the kind of pain that morphine
can't numb
and in spite of a societal anesthetic and deadening,
this pandemic seems to have no cure
We have a better chance of curing cancer than healing the
deadbeatedness of a man

Reprobate hearts don't beat
They are emotionless to the heart that beats through them
And though deaf ears can still hear muted sounds,
the deafness of a man who ignores the cries of his child,
a man that is absent from his biological rights
can't – no won't- no ignores the sounds of this being he
created
Let's be clear, not every man suffers from this pathology

Not every father is a carrier of this contagion
yet we are all affected if not infected by those that choose to
annihilate our communities
with their blatant disregard for the wellbeing
or the psychological and emotional health of our children
And it seems like every time a single mother writes about a
deadbeat father,
she shows up as the image of a woman scorned
A mad black woman whose man has moved on
But this, this isn't about him as my man
because that ship, that ship, like the titanic, has sailed
Yes! I'm angry!
I'm angry because my child wants a father,
and not just any father, he wants him
even as a child- he recognizes the synchronized cadences of
their hearts
As a child, he sees the value in connecting with the source
that gave him life
even if the source itself doesn't find value in sowing himself
into his own posterity
The boy is ready, willing, and asking to teach the elder
to be a man,
to be a father,
to be his father
and yes, to let the boy be a father to the man
 The progeny is offering the predecessor a chance to live his
life as a rebirth,

to un-ring a bell that was rung wrong,

reverse any generational curses,

and establish a legacy that will live throughout the ages

And I, as the mother,

I am forced to stand by this allegorical bedside

and watch my child fight for his life

Wait for packages in the mail as if his life depended on it

Believe every promise,

hide every disappointment,

and believe the next promise again

in hopes that this time, this time, this promise,

This tidbit of hope will not fail him

And yet it fails him.

It fails him!

And just like the elder man must have been taught by a

broken and heartless man-boy,

my boy-man tucks away the rejection

and God, I pray my son doesn't do what his father is doing

and pass this genetic disability on to his own children

You see, I want my son to look in the mirror

and see sanctification in his reflection

and not the abandonment and rejection he sees

when he searches for a three-dimensional reflection

in the person of a man

that reflects his own insecurities, shortcomings, and

inadequacies

because that's all he can see in his own obscured and
depreciated self-reflection

And so, I teach my son faith
but I can't teach him to pray like a man
I can't teach him how to cover and carry his family
spiritually
because God didn't create me to be the head
So how do I as the helpmeet for a man teach the child who
will one day be the head?
how to be the head if there is no head in his family or his
home?

And I teach him how to ride a bike
and I do it just like my Daddy did it
When he falls, I say, "Get back up, brush yourself off, and
get back on that bike"
but it's not the same
I'm still Mommy wanting to be soft and gentle
I want to put a band aid on it
I want to protect him
And hold him and shelter him from the next fall
but instead I have to put my baby back on that bike,
knowing all along that the bike riding lesson isn't really
about a bike at all,
it's about life

and so, I can't be Daddy, teaching his son the lessons of
life-
instead, I'm Mommy
I'm Mommy trying to be hard and soft at the same time
And why wouldn't our men be confused about their roles in
our society?
Because now Mommies are Daddies and Daddies want to
be Mommies
and that's a different poem
because I just want my son to be a confident man
and not a makeshift or shade-tree man
his mother pieced together
because his natural example of a man chose to sit this one
out

And so, I teach him how to tie a tie
and how to talk to girls
and he tells me about his first crush
and it robs him of his rites of passage as a young boy
as I'm sure his father must have been robbed
Surely, he never experienced the pride of his father
watching him dress for milestone events
Or maybe a man never explained to him how to treat girls
so that when he was a man,
he would know how to treat a woman
And if by chance he watched the maltreatment of his own
mother

and erroneously thinks he turned out ok
I rebuke the notion that my child will be a part of that inheritance

And while I see to my sons every need
I can be all things to him
but I still can't be man enough for what he needs
There's no gender reassignment to assuage an incurable condition
And though I walk through fire
and I scale tall buildings
and I would walk on water if I had to
I cannot make a man
I can't convince an incorrigible man to be a father
any more than I can show an optimistic and expectant boy how to be a man
I can't instill in him the seeds of knowledge that comes from a father
Even on my worst days, I'm more man than a father that won't support his own child
And though I do everything the way I learned it from my own father,
I'm still not man enough for what he needs

There's a vicious plague that has infected our communities.

So, we find ourselves in an outbreak

An undeniable, irrefutable epidemic
There is a systematic disregard by perpetrators
boys pretending to be men
doing men things,
with deep voices, full bodies, and facial hair
using boy tactics to shirk their responsibility
They simply take no exception to their children
And close at hand is their accessory; the carrier
the mothers who have fallen for the bait and switch
time and time and time again
And the biggest casualty?
It's not the determined mother who will try
in spite of her best efforts to be the father that the
biological man won't be
and it's not the absentee pater*
riddled and plagued with trifle
The biggest casualty is the child who doesn't know the
difference.
It's the boy who longs and hopes for the attention of the
man he wants so desperately to be accepted by
not knowing that that man hasn't even accepted himself
for the gift he has been given
It's the pubescent adolescent that will hold it all in
and lose the innocence of wanting and needing the
recognition of a father
that tells him he'll be a man yet
and feigns indifference when his world depends on it,

relies on it,
and can't be complete without it

This disease is a parasite to society
This disease is a callous and vile virus
It robs its objects of their choice or method of survival
and places an early and grim prognosis on their lives
It delivers a DO NOT RESUSCITATE to their childhood
and it attacks their immune system
It makes them vulnerable to the other, less debilitating
ailments that life carries
There is indeed a vicious and brutal plague
that is running rampant in our communities
The only antidote is a clear and present inoculation of
manhood
into those that would-be fathers,
an injection of fatherhood into the hearts and souls
of those that have walked away from their seed,
and an immunization against such atrocities
for the legacy of those that suffer the sicknesses of their
fathers today

*Absentee pater: Absent father

An Empty Poem

Empty
That hungry feeling you get
when you know you've just eaten
The notion that you're lost
when you think you're exactly where you're supposed to be
The lonely feeling you get
the frustration of loneliness
while amidst your loved ones

EMPTY IS A FRAME OF MIND!

Empty
The notion that you're extremely bored
when you've got a million and six things to do
Making a things-to-do list
and not fulfilling a single task
Anticipation, then nothing
Soul searching- only to be a stranger to yourself
Compassion, bonding, friendship
and then desperation in a time of need

EMPTY IS A PHASE OF LIFE!

Empty,

Holding on to the intangible
reaching out for the unreachable
Face to face, telepathic mind waves
languages of body, sign, and tongue
Still yet never understanding

EMPTY IS A STAGE OF LOVE!

Empty is my cup of fulfillment
Not half empty, not half full
Empty is faith without believing
Empty is the theatre of my soul,
And empty are the cheers and standing ovations that
applaud my every endeavor
Empty is knowledge without acknowledgement
Empty are the windows to my soul!
Empty are the bends at the ends of my lips
Empty is a subconscious phase that
walks us through the halls of life and love

Empty can be full,
but...
    Full can never be empty!

SMOKE

Who Do You See?

As I stand before you in plain view,
What do you see when you look at me?
Has society defined my image
 or created a cultural montage?
If you're looking, tell me, what is it you see?

From royalty and warrior bloodlines I come,
African and Native American
through my skin to my hair and in my veins
Indigenous and aboriginal in part
and somewhat foreigner at best
For my ancestors immigrated in chains
Who do you see?

My ancestral lineage is Biblically documented
from the beginning of time
I'm a Motherland descendant,
the product of a slave's reality
My ancestors' credits include the pyramids, mathematics,
and the sciences
I have a natural affinity for excellence
and the indwelling of a free man's mentality
Who do you see?

Granddaughter to a woman, who could bear no child,
And an heiress to my father's throne
As angels, they fly freely and watch over me
So, when you see me singularly, know I'm blessed and
never alone
Who do you see?

Do you see Dante', Gibran, Shange, Maya, or Giovanni?
Or perhaps you see one who pens a best-selling book
Per chance you see creativity, originality,
ingenuity, and a visionary
If not, focus in, my friend, take a look
Who do you see?

Do you see sincerity and benevolence
or a quiet peaceful demeanor?
A habitation of love that's rooted in faith
Do you see a person whom,
to date has yet to meet a stranger?
And still believes there's hope for the human race
Who do you see?

Now see my scars, my flaws, and imperfections
They're medallions of honor
to substantiate the unfairness of life
From battles fought, some won, some loss,
and some forfeited;

With my blood, sweat, and tears, a usual price
Who do you see?

I am artist and writer a carpenter and seamstress,
Building poetic bridges
and quilting a literary future from my past
I am servant and leader and an advocate for the defeated
A motivator and a teacher of my craft
Who do you see?

I am Mike Brown, Trayvon Martin, Sandra Bland,
Marissa Alexander, and Kelly Williams-Bolar
I am Emmett, Nat Turner, Rosa, Garvey, and Angela too
I am Martin, I am Malcolm, Michelle,
Douglass, Carver, and Dubois
And if you fail to see the connection, one day I'll be you too
Who do you see?

I speak with signs that are sacred and clandestine
I speak with languages from many tongues
and a different land
I speak with prudence and compassion,
a universal language to all
And I speak for diversity and the multitude of man
Chi vede?
Qui voyez vous?
A quien ves?

Whetin' you dey see Oh?
Who do you see?

I am proud of this junction to which life has brought me
Please take note of my poise, stature, and stance
Through the Refiners fire, I've journeyed
and will go again and again
Not something you'll see if at first only you glance
Who do you see?

Though my layers may seem minimal,
superficial and unsophisticated,
And what your eyes see appears to be quite clear
Seeing me with naked eyes and only your vision,
Is like having ears without listening to what you hear
Tell me, who do you see?

This Little Light of Mine

I

This little light of mine, I'm going to let it shine

This little light of mine, I'm going to let it shine

This little light of mine, I hid it under a basket of refuge

This basket is the smile that says all is well,

A pretense of confidence when I'm not too sure myself.

I hide my light when I feel my trust has been breached

Creating a barrier protecting me from heartaches

and disappointments

Unfortunately, hindering me from true love

and doubt-free relationships.

I seem durable, care free, and witty,

nonchalant, outspoken, and speaking out

With a ride or die outer shell on the surface

But I am shy and often quite sensitive

My wounded self peaks out without my permission

I am simplistically complex and confusingly cumbersome

The more my light transforms and adjusts,

The heavier what I really hold gets,

and the harder it is to maintain

II.

One time I loved so hard I lost myself

It was a childhood love affair.

A love that now spans well into adulthood
With every I love you, my light got brighter
Then after years of "I love you", there was never a goodbye,
And now it's "I still love you",
Something happened to me.
I learned that S-O-U-L mate
Was really only an S-O-L-E mate

III
On my 19th birthday, a day to celebrate my shine,
When I should have been sneaking and tiptoeing
Through my college sweetheart's dorm;
I lost the first man I ever loved
The first man that gave me proof that he would die
before his love for me died.
I sat at his funeral and begged him not to leave me
He could leave the others, I swore,
But if he left me there would be no need for this shell of me
Without him, my light would not need to shine
His legacy became my foundation.
I became a basket case,
A young girl who has lost her father
Or loses this little light of mine
before she experiences true love
Is a recipe for failed love in the future.

IV

There were times when my light became intensely bright,

This little light of mine

Times I let it shine,

Moments and flashes of success

Friendships that last a light-time

And memories that somehow

still bring laughter and smiles

And since one can never be too careful,

I just keep everything under my basket

And somehow, the good times and the happy moments

Mix with the darker ones

Like a proverbial melting pot.

V

One Christmas eve,

I sat with my Grandmother, this light of mine

We laughed and talked for hours

"Write a book," she told me. "Put it all on paper"

"Marry this kind of man." She said

"One minute, you're like Einstein,

The next minute you're a fucking Jerry Lewis poster child,"

She would say.

 "Don't be a Jerry Lewis poster child."

"Everything in life comes with warning signs,"

"Before there's fire, there's always smoke

And there are always clouds before there's rain.

Don't ignore the warning signs," she forewarned

I don't know why she told me this that night.

There was no other place I wanted to be

on a Christmas Eve at 26 years old

Than hanging with my best girlfriend

She was my inspiration and my light source

She brought meaning and added wisdom

And a purpose to my light

We shared everything

She knew the inventory of my basket

The noble, contrite, dreadful, and the indifferent

There were no secrets- except the one she kept

And tried to prepare me for that Christmas Eve

By Christmas morning,

My grandmother's illuminated light left me.

I wanted to die with her but she left too much for me to do,

Too much to share, too much to write

And though it was a dim and shadowy time of my life

She fed my light and continues to feed me

I hide that because sharing her felt like betrayal

I thought the light she left would eventually run out

But you just can't hide Hazel Franks.

I was poster childish enough to think

That there wasn't enough of her light to go around

So, she became a part of what I hold in my basket

And I hide behind her even as I share my light today.

VI
I have travelled the world and saw things
That most don't see in a light-time
I held audience, rubbed shoulders
Dined with the wealthiest
I worked for a man who on a whim
Purchased a strip of the Atlantic coastline,
villages included
I volunteered at an orphanage in an African village,
Fed fresh mangos to a healthy baby girl
named Who-Knows,
A shortened version of
Who Knows What Tomorrow Brings
This little light of mine,
left to die in the darkness of a sewer,
She will always be a radiant
and resplendent point of my life
I cried for a man that had been lying dead
For two days on a busy Nigerian road
As cars passed him by and people on foot
Covered their faces and crossed the street,
This little light of mine dimmed
I mourned for a stranger;
I prayed for his soul and still pray,
Till this day, that his dying will not be in vain
Whether my light grew brighter or dim
My resolve strengthened my wick of life

What I carried and concealed on the inside,

Conceivably mirrored a corrupt,

Unforgiving, lonely, bitter,

Beautifully diverse, full of surprises,

And extremely perplexing world on the outside

VII

I put my reluctance to trust aside

And allowed vulnerability to grow within.

The kill switch on my light was fool proof

Or at least tested by fools

I fell in love and married

For better or for worse, till death do us part.

The better, worse, and death happened all at once.

At the apex of my life, I was in love

In the next moment,

I found myself putting two babies in one grave

I held and kissed my twins one by one

And I don't know if the light extinguished or exploded,

There's no darkness like a mother burying her babies

So, I cursed the light and what I had been holding within.

Damn both of them!

But darkness doesn't last always

After my darkest moment, my brightest,

Most brilliant moment came at 32 weeks,

As this little light of mine

Tossed and turned within me

I cleared out my heart for a new light-time of memories
In the fall of '04, the gleam in my eye was permanently
etched

VIII

Through the years, I continue to love and to live
At times, it feels like I've lost more than I've gained
It's hard to keep count
I stand before you as a basket toppled upright
And this little light of mine exposed
Leaving scorch marks as evidence of my losses and failures
Showing patches of spackling where I've kept my secrets

I can't hold what I carry and keep this little light of mine
Either I shine in freedom or I live in darkness
I embrace the newness of what life brings
or live in yesterday
There's a story to tell under this basket
The same basket I thought was protecting me
Was suffocating my light, this little light of mine
No more holding back my light
I will no longer be subdued by a basket
I have to let it shine - this beautiful light of mine
My basket is now ablaze, incinerated-
Giving new meaning to self-combustion
My light can only get so bright
Without eventually setting the basket on fire

I think I'll let it burn!
The haze you see is forgiveness,
That basket that once veiled this little light of mine
Now serves as a furnace-
Burning those things I can no longer hold,
Releasing billows of growth and change,
Slow smoldering with moments of happiness, joy and love
Emitting an aroma of inner-peace
Giving off whiffs of the wisdom of life
And memories I'll cherish for a light-time.
Aromatherapy for the woman I'm becoming each day
This little light of mine, I am going to let it shine
That basket that once sheltered my light, let it burn
This little light of mine, I am going to let it shine
Let it shine! Let it shine! Let it shine!

A Letter to My Heart

To Whom It May Concern,

Please accept this letter as a formal complaint with regard to your capricious, reckless, and irresponsible method of handling your affairs. Statistically and historically, such behavior has created a burden for our department. Many hours have been spent deciphering your intentions when the most prudent thing to do would be to dispatch, remit, relegate, and or consign such undertakings with this division. While it is understandable that you would consider dealing with such issues in-house, it is advisable if not judicious that you simply cease and desist any efforts to determine or resolve any interpersonal concerns where feelings and emotions might be involved. Should you have any questions or concerns, or require any additional information, please know that the CCU (Cerebral Concern Unit) has already taken them into consideration as we are the point of origin for all questions and concerns.

Sincerely,

The Brain

The Heart Responds:

Dear Brain,

First and foremost, it is a pleasure, as always, to hear from

you. I pray that this letter finds you in the best of health
and free of calamity and bewilderment.

Of course, I understand and appreciate your concerns. I
assure you, however, such concerns are best dealt with in
this department. I am sure I don't need to remind you that
emotional matters or matters of the heart can't be resolved
with statistics, historical data, and or reason in some cases
Thank you for your efforts, but for the best interest of our
carrier, I will continue to handle the more sensitive affairs.
Again, it is a pleasure hearing from you. We should
communicate and correspond more often. May your days
be filled with kindness, peace, and liberty.

Lovingly,

The Heart

The Brain Responds:

To Whom It May Concern;

It is my understanding that you insist on handling what
you refer to as the more sensitive affairs. Your track record
of such issues is not remarkable. I have watched you get
battered and beaten emotionally, heartbroken, and simply
abused. Continuously, you accept people who I am sure are
not acting in OUR best interest, yet you waste compassion,
causing this department to expend energy on individuals
that do not return your sentiments.

Additionally, you have placed this department in a position
of wonder when relating to interpersonal relationships. I

cannot emphasize enough the fact that romance and affection are intangible thoughts generated by you. I am not able to control the thoughts that are generated by your department and therefore am unable to sever or terminate such thoughts.

Please be advised, effective immediately, if you insist on handling such matters lackadaisically, and without reservations, I will no longer assist you by withholding your feelings and reminding you of past hurts and fears. Furthermore, if you continue to challenge my expertise in these areas, I completely withdraw from all matters of the heart and you will be forced to deal with such issues without the cooperation and involvement of this department.

The Brain

The Heart Responds:

Dear Brain,

Again, it is a pleasure to hear from you. Your views are always welcome. I assure you, that though I have, in fact, experienced some rather difficult times; I have had more pleasant and joyful times than I can count. I find solace in knowing that there are so many wonderful experiences waiting for me. I pray that you will observe closely so that you too can enjoy such blessings.

As for the condition of this department, the tears and cracks add character. The foundation of this department is love. The walls are lined with compassion and there is a bright light that glows within. Yes, there have been some unforeseeable mishaps and even devastation, but every time, I somehow regenerate and am filled with a presence even stronger than before.

Brain, what you see, from your perspective, may not look good. I assure you, I am in excellent condition, the best ever.

Finally, I accept your letter of resignation from my affairs, effective immediately. I have been waiting to hear this for quite some time

Lovingly,

The Heart

Controller of All Things Good

Heirloom Tides

I've walked a million miles and crossed oceans
I have even drowned in them
I've lost my babies
My tears are the high tide
I've carried and still carry other babies on my back,
Carefully tying knots to secure their dreams and their
future
My mind plays and replays phrases and words
That I don't care to recall or maybe I have not yet heard
My pen moves incessantly
My eyes are my ink and my heart is the paper
I collect words, praying to unearth the perfect poem
for peculiar situations
I am a Motherland experience
infused with fragmented cultures
I am Saturday morning, hair grease
and pressing comb certified
Big Mamma's Night Musk mixed with Catawba
Reservation red dirt
And the sounds of a summer revival
provide incense and a soundtrack for my craft
Summers in Pontiac, Michigan
and sleepovers with older cousins introduced me

To Pink Champale, cussing, and eyeliner;

Tools for some of life's most essential moments

I am macaroni and cheese and collard greens

I am cassava, suya, and foo-foo

I am sushi and tiramisu

I am the indispensable esoteric pull me up,

A literary docent

My libretto sings the songs of my ancestors,

Hums the tunes of their passage,

And engraves my story in the walls of a legacy

built on foundations of strength and hope

My life is the braille of those whose shoulders I stand on

My existence is the sign language for the voices that were

silenced

And the words that were never spoken

I am humbly gifted with a burden,

My pen moves incessantly

cataloging my testimonies of this life

My eyes are the tear-moistened ink within a quill

that never dries and never stops asking

My heart is my paper where sentiment and words hold

communion and poems are born

Angels edit my experiences

God is my Publisher on High

My unwritten poems are the sounds of raindrops on a tin

roof,

Falling lyrically in my thoughts and dreams

For these poems, I'll walk another million miles
Its low tide and I labor for the birth of the poems
That are happening around me

A Poem in My Heart

When I was a child
I kept a smile in my pocket
but now,
I have a poem in my heart
And I can't get it out

There's a poem in my heart
a sentiment
an emotion that words alone won't sustain
a yearning to tell a story
this rhapsody without music in my heart

On the other side of this darkness
I can meet my creative persona
In the morning when the sun finally rises
and the moon will release its' hold
In a new day, I'll try to explain
this saga in my soul

Yesterday,
I had a twinkle in my eye,
today, I see a shadow of doubt
I have a poem in my heart

and I can't get it out

Though my creativity has gone AWOL
and my ingenuity is malfunctioning
I still sense an inclination to divulge
this frame of reference on my mind

Like an accident waiting to happen
better said, a child waiting to be born
Yet neither asking to exist
and still,
there's a poem in my heart
and I can't get it out

This morning there was a ringing in my ear
I could hear all of the things I hold inside
I could feel them breaking down
the walls of reluctance and anxiety
this verse in my heart
that I cannot create

I have a song in my mind
and no words of which to sing
I am a dancer with no rhythm
and a poet without a poem

When I was a child

I kept a smile in my pocket

but now,

I have a poem in my heart

and can't get it out

Confessions
(Written 5/11/2009)

In my life, I want to fulfill my needs
I want to reach my fullest extent
I want to see at my visions fullest potential
And hear the words of the most knowledgeable elders
In every tongue- with total understanding

This I desire

I want to walk a straight line with my friends
And never cross that fine line with my enemies
I want to love unselfishly
And accept love in return,
Unexpecting and with gracious consent

This I want

I want to know with blessed assurance
that I am not the only one to have traveled this path
I want to know that with a mustard seed of faith
Surely, I too will make it through
And surely, this is not new only to me

This I pray

As I weave my tangled web,
May I not fall prey to my own deceit
And should vengeance become my purpose,
Any weapon formed against me,
May it not prosper

This is my request

I want to be self-sufficient in my every endeavor
Otherwise efficient in everything I do
I want my actions and concerns to evoke proficiency
By me as well as those I reach

This I mandate

I resolve to demonstrate conviction in my creeds
Whereas denounce bliss where ignorance is concerned
 I resolve to build dreams upon bases of reality
Thus, maintaining goals that are not only attainable
But tangible and purposeful as well

This is my volition

May I hold true to all of my aspirations

Never fall short of that which I perceive to be the
necessities of life

For these will be my confessions

I Love Her

I love her.
Not that perverted love or the kind of love that has never
been defined by Webster or Roget
This love is the kind of love created in spiritual realms
Undefinable, everlasting
This is that resonates within every fiber of your being,
kind of love
It's a love I already knew and I still want to know
Call it kismet; call it organic, or a kindred kind of love
I love her.
Our first encounter was story book ready
It was that out of body, love at first sight type of love
She was colorful
The kind of colors Crayola can't duplicate or name
Her mood and aura says festive
But I know that she holds numerous stories of hurt and
pain
Of losses and of abuse
She bears the weight of generations on her shoulders
She is the Daughter of the Mother of Civilization
One could easily call her the original Big Mamma
or the Auntie of the world
She is the mother of stolen nations

The Niger and the Delta Rivers are the result of her tears
for her lost and miscarried babies
She clashes with the Atlantic for her children whom she
knows though they may never know her
This is that deep love, that bottom of the ocean love
She holds and embraces me
Her arms are like branches of the Iroko tree
She knows my people and my people's people
She speaks different languages
and somehow in her presence, I understand them all
I am consumed by her fragrances
and enthralled by her movement
I love her.
This love is in the nucleus of my being,
it is predestined love
She says it's okay to be me
She makes me proud of my physical attributes
And celebrates the way my nose is rounded on three sides
without angles
And the way my bottom lip seems to smile more than my
top lip because one is fuller than the other
She appreciates the melanin in my skin
And the way my locs are like the roots of my family tree-
strong, natural,
Without the need of explanation or justification,
untamable but certainly all mine
Our love is locked and she is the key

This is that love a mother has at first sight of her baby

In this love, I am the new birth

She is a secret keeper

She bears the secrets of millions of souls

spread across her diaspora

Her ankles are shackled for those impoverished,

lost, or stolen spirits

This is that heavy, I've got your back kind of love

Her smile is sunshine

She is radiant and opulent

She is a proud creature

Not the puffed-up pride but well-deserved dignity and

nobility

She is drenched in aristocracy

Kings and Queens, then and now, hail from her grace

I love her.

This is royal love

I love her perfected dysfunction

and her dysfunctional perfection

With her, I am home

The chaotic peace in my mind makes sense

With her, creativity is limitless and without boundaries

She is sound, touch, taste, and smell

She awakens my senses

Our love is a conscious and stimulating type of love

I love her.

This isn't fad, pop culture,

or a convenient infatuation or admiration
This is a forever kind of love
She is Africa.
She is Nigeria.
This is that perfect love
She is a ballad to the poet
Her story is written by Time and Nature
and narrated by the stars and the moon
She speaks in iambic meter
Her heartbeat is the rhythm of the dancer
And the songbirds jazz and blues
I love her.
I am certain, she loves me too.

RAIN

Consider Love
(ACF, Albion, NY 10/3/2011)

Take away the hope and the wonder
Of this magical moment turned fairy tale
And never question what the future holds
Or if this fool-proof plan could ever fail

Pray for what we see and not our wishes
Live in the moment as it stands
Count only on ourselves as resources
Would we trust it in our own hands?

Ignore statistics and scientific deductions
Exclude history and previous acclaims
Relying just on what's brought to this table
Has love always found honor in our names?

Accepting the much that's required of us
Seeking a justified and reasonable share
Living simply by life's intricate handbook
and knowing fully, it's not always fair

So, I pray and I question and wonder
For a love that's unfettered and free

That this vision of love we've given life to
Is not visible only to me

Don't think for one moment I've faltered
Or reconsidered the plans for our life
Just know I leave nothing unthought of
It's my duty as your friend, lover, and wife

Loving You with All of Me

With my mind
Because you are in my thoughts everyday
You are on my mind
Your scent, your walk, your smile
The way you touch me and hold me in your arms
The comfort I feel when you hold my hand
And the protection I feel in your presence
It is with my mind that I love you

With my body
When I touch your face to wipe away a tear
And hold your hand
Or stand by your side
When I am holding you in my arms
The smile that comes to life
The butterflies in my stomach when I see you
Watching you sleep, making sure you are warm
And holding you tight
When I'm making love to you
The way our bodies become one
I love you with my body

With my heart
There's a place in my heart
Reserved just for you
It's the way I want to chase away your fears
And take away the pain
I want to protect you from the cruelty of this world
And create a haven of love fit for you
It's with compassion, honesty, sincerity, and tenderness
I love you with my heart

With my soul
In sickness and in health
For richer and for poorer
With my vows and in my prayers
In the blessedness of Holy matrimony
Praying that God will make me
What you need in a friend
A sister, a lover, and a wife
With spiritual alignment
And the power of prayer

I love you with my mind,
My body,
My heart,
And my soul
I love you all ways and
I love you always

Love's Timing

Sometimes

not often

we love so hard

we become blind

to the most important aspects of our relationship

we can only remember

the gentle kisses

tight hugs

snuggled nights

and cuddled mornings

At times

occasionally

there were hard times

big disagreements

heated discussions

and condescending remarks

but we never forgot

the good times

the long walks

the nights alone

late night ice cream

and early morning cheese and crackers

then there were

the long-winded apologies

Too often
they followed the hard times
The gentle kisses
tight hugs
and snuggled mornings
became too scarce
Most of the time
and too often
we forgot that
sometimes
it's hard to love the way we should
Continually
we lost sight of the fact that
sorry isn't enough and
I love you is just a sentence
if not backed by emotion
An occasional hardship
is the same as a chronic disease
always in the way
and usually blinding
Generally
we forgot
our only destination and purpose was
to always be in love
always be happy
and to never cause the other pain
not even sometimes

because that would have been too often

You Were Worthy

You were worthy of a poem of articulate emotions
Serenaded with no respect to rhyme or reason
You were regarded with passion and patience
Like a garden that would flourish in due season

You were worthy of the secrets I keep well hidden
It's not a package too many would see
Yet you misappraised my thoughts, dreams, hopes, and
fears
And missed a chance to know the authentic and genuine
me

You were worthy of estimable attention
For your acts of kindness and reflective deeds
You were applaudable for just being worthy
And that alone filled some of my needs

Your esteemed value and meritable position
Now find me doubtless and faithless in you
And that garden now renders a defunct harvest
Where sincerity and harmony grew

Your refusal to acknowledge my value
and your negligence in reverencing this Queen

May appear to deflate my hopes for higher horizons
But are undignified and theoretically obscene

Your attempts to adulterate and debase me
Your disrespect with words to demean
Were inept as they fell to fallow ground
Because this diamond would not lose her sheen

So, in spite of your intentions and plummeting value
You've yielded a seed that will continue to grow
But don't think you've escaped without consequence
Cause in life, you must reap what you sow

And while your worth has depreciated in its' merit
A once thriving garden is now inhospitable and bleak
That which lives, may be cut down, yet it will still live again
And the invaluable seed that I'll sow in a new foundation of
worth
In its' own due season, will peak!

Lost and Found

I waited for you to find me/ like a peacock, I displayed my
array of beauty before you / I paraded my virtuosity,
praying you would recognize the possibility/ or simply
acknowledge that I am a rare sight to see/ but you didn't
see me/ And that's understandable because I couldn't see
myself/ I was so determined to be your corrective lens/
that I lost myself in the hopes that I'd fit in/ and be what
you were looking for.

The truth is I've been lost for a long time/ I got so wrapped
up in wanting you to find me that I lost myself in the vision
I was sure would define me/ I thought I needed to recreate
an oasis/ so that you could relate to the benefaction and
reward that stood before you/ while I attempted to
redesign me/ I found that your hang ups and limitations
and a necessitated external validation would only confine
me/ and somehow, I lost sight of who I am.

I assumed you'd see that I am a princess because my father
decreed it/ and a Queen because life experiences and time
have ordained me/ please don't keep asking for your fair
share of peace and happiness/ when the answer stood
before you and was plain to see/ and I lost me / My reign

doesn't exist to intimidate, debilitate, emasculate, or even Infiltrate/ I find joy in supporting my king and building an empire together.

I thought that once you saw my natural crown/ you'd see my natural beauty/ my inherent charm/ my built-in intellect/ and know that ONLY God can create this masterpiece/ And I lost me like a child wandering away from her mother's grip/ I felt incomplete and ineffectual in my own interpersonal relationship/ I lost me in the rhetorical montage I was willing to become.

I lost my belief in fairy tales/ waiting for a happily ever after/ when my once upon a time self-divided and has been more frequent than I care to recount/ because I've realized that each of my defects and imperfections somehow allowed you an ethical discount/ and it began to diminish my self-esteem in astronomical amounts/ and in ways that I can't even count/ and finding me right now is paramount.

I looked into your windows/ wondering if in vulnerability, I had lost myself in you/ but I wasn't in the trophy case/ on a pedestal/ in your pocket/ or riding shot gun/ I'm not your ride or die because I'll choose my life every time/ and to think, like Hansel and Gretel, I left morsels of myself/ knowing that if you could, O' taste and see my goodness/

but I couldn't find me through your windows/ because you couldn't see me for who I am.

I lost me/ and this is your loss/ I get that I am damaged goods/ and truthfully, I'm damaged good/ and damn I'm good/ because even when I was lost, I was still winning/ In losing me, I found resilience and perseverance/ I found strength and joy in just being me.

I lost me and found myself / Not in a lost and found box or sitting idle on a shelf/ There were no posters to highlight my absence/ I found what you should be looking for/ I found a deeper love for myself.

I found me.

Touch Me

Touch me. Touch me. Feel me. Hold me.
Ahhh, touch me.
Touch me with your tongue, not your taste buds
but touch me with your words.
Don't make them long,
there's no need for offensively sweet.
Just make them yours and touch me with your thoughts;
Sincere words that hold my heart
and deep words that engage my mind.
Yeah, that's it. Touch me right there.
Touch me with your eyes.
And not because you look at me, but let your eyes see me.
Look into my eyes and let's talk I to I, touch to touch,
silently.
See my desire and my pleasure,
let your eyes touch me gently and touch me deep.
Touch me with an indescribable touch.
Touch me with your spirit, the inner you.
Let the man that hides behind the shining armor touch me.
Massage my spirit in ways
that only heaven can comprehend.
Touch me until emotion-filled tear drops well.

Let my spirit in
so our spirits can bear witness to each other.
Hold me in your arms,
not with your strength or because your arms can reach,
Embrace me with your you-ness
and pull me into your personal space.
Let your scent take residence in my mind.
Secure me in your shelter and shelter me in your security.
Touch me. Yes! Touch me.
Touch me with your hands.
Squeeze my hands in yours
as you lead us to a different place.
Take me to your sanctuary, your place.
Guide me that I may see you too,
Catch me and redirect me when I stumble.
Touch me with tenderness. Baby me with intimacy.
Touch my feelings. Caress my mind.
Surround my senses and indulge my inner sensitivities.
Handle me with masculinity,
a strong gentleness and a gentle firmness.
Don't be shy. Touch me with compliments;
The kind that words can't speak.
Touch me. Touch me.
Touch me with your trust and handle mine with care.
Feel the delicacy of my inhibitions
as they slide through your fingers.
Touch me. Touch all of me.

It's in how you embrace and feel and caress me
that you'll know you've really touched me.
And when you touch me like this...
Ahhhh! When you really touch me,
that's when you'll know
I've been touching you all along
Touch me!

The Redemption of Love

When I was a child, I spoke as a child
I loved
As a child, I would without question or reluctance
spread my arms wide
Love was my playground
and I embraced its fascinating tide
Lackadaisically and pretentiously, I played with cupid
Unaware of his stature
and the roll he'd come to play in my life
Time has taught me that love's playground
isn't always a pleasant place to play
An uneven terrain and rusted tools
produce broken hearts, egos that are bruised,
and obstacles that become giants
First sight love affairs become myths
An old childhood playmate becomes elusive, oppositional,
and quite often defiant
For as sure as I find it I am assured this love could cease
Those that dare engage despise and contemn their pursuit
of love
Fearful of the pitiable and ejective outcomes,
I believe in and seek that which I cannot hold and that
which I cannot release

And still I search
It is clear; I am in love with love
Regrettably, love doesn't always return the sentiment
And now I seek him
 I yearn for him
and envision the day that love will seek me too
Throw himself uncontrollably into my proclivities
as lovers are often wont to do
Impatiently, I wait for love to bring back butterfly kisses,
holding hands, and star gazing
Restore the fantasies of enraptured evenings
Design a smile that's made for me
Deliver him to me and place me at his heart
Render me indefensible under his protection
unshakable when he seeks my refuge
and my circumspection
I will cover him in prayer
and strengthen and nourish his body and mind
For him I will be uninhibited
releasing and vanquishing my guard
I will meet him in spiritual realms
and take flight in galaxies
only traversed by love and angels and God
I will cherish his secrets and encourage his dreams
Giving birth to visions that he may see – but I will believe
Love, is it that you redeem me- or Love, do I redeem thee?
Have I not paid a price?

Through sickness and in death – I still loved
In ascension and discourse – on this playground called life,
I found trust in you when I could trust no other
When I was loved by others and couldn't love myself-
I found healing by giving that same love I so desperately
needed to someone else
It's as if I have offended you
and dare to ask you to reveal yourself
What else must I forfeit
that I've not already given for your return
Have I not endured a kaleidoscope of emotions
in hopes that there would be an abstract moment
where Love and I could abide and cohabitate?
Have I not given myself to your unpredictable enigmas?
Am I not afraid of your wrath and desolation?
Do I not stand in fear of your absence
and how it produces disconcerting stigmas?
Will you release my love?
Or is it that his love will be your proxy?
Acceptance in his sight and forgiveness in yours,
Is this plausible for my flaws?
Or have my temporal professions of eternal love
disqualified me from your redemption
and found me in contempt and condescension
of loves' intricate and often inequitable laws?
Is it lofty of me
to desire a love like Ozzie Davis and Ruby Dee?

And with what degree of reverence do I approach you to
ask-
Do I presume to redeem love
Or is it that Love, you redeem me?

Clouds Before Fire And Smoke Before Rain

The Tempest is Raging

PROLOGUE
PEACE BE STILL!

The Tempest is Raging
PROLOGUE
PEACE BE STILL!

Lavina sat pensively in the back of the family car with tears streaming down her face, meeting at her chin, and cascading down her blouse. Though she heard noises, she could not talk or respond. Her mind was blank and yet, there was a torrent of activity at the same time. Her heart was filled with anguish. Life can't be this way. She wanted to holler. She wanted to just fall out, act a fool and beg, "Dear Lord, this can't be. Why God? How could you let this happen?" She wanted to curse the thought that this was a forgiving God. A loving God. The more her mind raced, the less she could say. She sat and let the tears roll down her face. She could remember the times they would play and the times they would argue. Though she was only three years older than her sister, Lavina was the proud big sister. She had always been told that she had to do the right thing because her younger siblings were watching her. Somehow, as they got older, the tables turned and Lavina found herself envying her younger sister and wanting to be like her.

The car rounded the corner and Lavina almost smiled at the thought; the thought of hating Malaika. Her emotions welled in the pit of her stomach and surfaced to her throat. She felt as if she wouldn't survive this moment. Her body was numb and she felt as if she were having a terrible out of body experience. Just to make sure that this was real, that this wasn't a cruel joke being played by fate, she clenched her teeth down on the insides of her cheeks until the feeling came back again. She took a deep swallow to move the lump in her throat around, for reassurance that she wasn't the only one feeling this way. She finally glanced away from the window to study the other passengers in the family car. She caught her brother Malik's' eyes, but could not stand the sight of him. What she saw was Malaika, his "guardian angel" as he called her. She choked for air to keep what little composure she had left as she continued to look at each of the passengers in the car. It was the look on their mother's face that she was not prepared for.

Ayanna was having the worst day of her life. Well she thought that, but it had been a bad week, a bad month, a bad year. She thought to herself, "Life just can't be this way for one person." She was lethargic and sluggish. But it was the look on her face that scared her other children. Inside, Ayanna didn't know whether to laugh or cry. She just couldn't remember which emotion went with what she was feeling. Was this a graduation, a dance recital, or was she just on her way to pick her youngest daughter up from school? And what was the big deal; anyway? Why was

Lavina so persistent that she wear these clothes? And where did Malik come from? She was sure that she hadn't seen him in months. It was an argument in which she had banned her only son from her own house. She knew that. And she knew that the only time he had even attempted to come back was because Malaika had begged him to.

Malaika could get Malik to do anything. They were best friends, brother and sister. They practically raised each other. Malik was so stubborn and if he had his mind set on something, come hell or high water, even if it looked like rain, he would not sway one way or the other. That is, of course, unless Malaika had something to do with it. Malaika, just like her name, was an angel. She stood her ground but she was diplomatic and compromising. She would smile and talk to you in just a way that you could not refuse the deed or task that she was asking. And it was Malaika who could convince her brother that her very own shit did not stink.

With so many favorable memories going through her mind, Ayanna stroked her son's hand. He was rigid and tense, like a corpse. His body was cold. She looked and saw his face wet with tears. His silk shirt and tie were tear soaked, or was it blood? She couldn't tell. Part of her could not understand why he was crying or if it were Malik, or Malaika sitting there. Ayanna was confused but she knew in her heart of hearts that if she would just let that pain that was bellowing at the pit of her stomach rise to the top, all of the answers to her questions would surface as well. She couldn't handle it. She wiped the tears from her child's' face and pulled him into her arms the way she did when he was a small boy. At first, he resisted. Everything was always a struggle with him these days but Malaika would see him and make him be reasonable with his mother. She patted his face again until he just collapsed into her arms and lap. He sobbed. Head bent and buried into his mothers' lap, he sobbed like a child.

Ayanna, in her infinite motherly ways, stroked his face, kissed the top of his head. "Honey, if you can't talk to me you can definitely tell Malaika... She'll be here after a while. She will be glad to see you here. You know she will." She struggled with what to say to calm him. Her best attempt was feeble at best, "I am certainly glad to see you." Ayanna continued rocking and stroking her son. She never realized that he was now sitting up and looking at her. There was rage and terror on his face. He was yelling something. She could hear him but she couldn't make out the words. Something about he was going and never coming back. He was hollering and beginning to frighten her. No, she couldn't understand her son, but she could feel the strength of his voice from the vibration in her soul. She filed this feeling along with the rest of the confusion that she felt.

"She's gone! She's gone!!! Mama! Damn, Malaika is dead. She's gone and she ain't gon' make nothing okay, cause she ain't coming back!!"

Malik was sitting upright like a soldier ready for battle. His sister was gone and now his mother was saying that she would make things ok. What was going on here? His best friend was gone and it was probably his fault. He let his face fall into his hands as he sobbed openly. Shoulders hovering and heaving, it was all he could do. For the first time in a long time, he did not have control of this situation. Malik sniffed and sat up. He wanted to be strong for his mother and sister. He wanted to be the man of the family. So many times they tried to force him to take charge and be the "The Man". There were even times when they would seemingly slide over and leave the head of the household position vacant just so that he would assume it himself. He couldn't. In a house full of strong and intelligent women, he was the lion without courage. Especially when it came to Malaika. She wouldn't go for any of his scheming, games, or simple lies. She would smile and laugh with him as if she were going along with whatever he was up to the whole while. Then she would pull his face to her and look him square in the eyes and say, "You shouldn't tell the strongest person the weakest lies."

He choked on the thought. He had told the weakest lie and she was dead because of it.

Malaika was his guardian angel. She knew him inside out. She trusted him, and likewise, he trusted her with his everything. It was Malaika that taught him to roller skate, tie his shoes, and even play basketball. She was honest. She was fair. She never cheated him in their games. She always put him before herself. Theirs was a special bond. Malaika was a giving person. She was an angel and more so, she was his true guardian angel and had been since birth. They had shared the same womb together for nine months. He was the bigger baby so he had been told. Malaika, feeble, weak, and cut off from any source of air supply, moved over anyway to let her brother out. It was later discovered that her lungs were underdeveloped, and she was underweight; all because the bigger baby took up all of the room and used most of the nourishment. She was in an incubator for weeks and constantly in the hospital for some reason or another. She had given of herself from before they were born and he had taken ungraciously. Malaika was not only his twin, she was his alter ego. They were in the same school together and the same classes all of their lives. They had the same opportunities but she was better. She was honest and pretty. She was someone to be proud of. She taught him most of what he knew. He had gotten involved with the wrong crew and life had been a bit bitter since then. Despite all of that, it was Malaika who still believed in him; who still loved him openly and unconditionally. She was the best thing that ever happened to him. And now she was there no more. He began to cry harder.

The car rounded the corner and pulled into the church parking lot. There were already tons of people there. He straightened his tie and tried to make reason with the already tear-stained tie and shirt. He looked at Lavina who obviously could not face him, then at his mother who had an indescribable look on her face. His heart stopped for her. He wanted to touch her but was afraid. He wanted to say, "Mama, you still have me." But in comparison to Malaika, he knew that would not be of any consolation. Instead, he bowed his head and obediently stepped from the car followed closely by his elder sister Lavina.

The flowers at the front of the church were vibrant as well as plentiful. There were white and pink roses arranged into a Princess Spray across the casket. There were lilies and orchids in almost every color at the head and foot of the casket. There was a large arrangement of bright fuchsia bleeding hearts mixed in with baby's breath and plants with colorful leaves and blooms. Several pews in the church were already filled. There was an audible whimper across the room. Dietrich Haddon's *Well Done* repeated over the sound system.

The procession line began to move with Ayanna directly behind the clergy. The line seemed to speed up and Ayanna wasn't quite sure what would happen once she got to the coffin. As if she were a child, she grabbed Lavina's hand and held it tightly. There were so many young children there hugging and crying with each other. "This must be one of their friends." She thought to herself. It was then that she saw her; her baby in the casket lying there peacefully. She was in such a deep sleep, Ayanna could not touch her. She just looked at her and watched her sleep as she had so many nights and years before. She patted the side of the casket and turned to the weeping eyes around her.

"She's such a good girl, and she's pretty too." Said a woman that she did not know.

"It's such a shame," the woman said. She patted Lavina's hand, "Lord be with you and your family. My family will keep y'all in our prayers. If you need anything," She emphasized the anything. "Just call the church office..." She seemed to go on and on.

Lavina smiled and said, "God bless you too."

As Lavina turned to concentrate on the image before her, all the feelings that had rumbled deep in her belly began to surface, and without warning she began to bellow. She cried. She fought as the funeral directors helped her to her seat next to her mother.

"No, God No!" She howled. "Oh my God! My baby sister is gone. God, no!" Her body went faint and she was on the floor. Ayanna looked down at her and could not speak nor move. She was shell shocked, speechless, and confused. She bowed her head and began to weep.

As Malik approached the casket with his twin lying so peacefully, his heart started to race. He wanted to touch her. He wanted to pick her up and hold her. He had so many things to say to her in saying his goodbyes. He approached her and gasped. It was himself he saw. Even as fraternal twins, people always commented on how much they looked alike. Malik never saw how much they resembled. There was never a time when they were mistaken for each other, but this time he may have done it himself. He backed away from her as if he had seen a ghost. That's what it was. He saw his own ghost. "No!" he yelled to no one in particular. He stumbled backward on to someone who pushed him back to her. There he was, once again staring at himself. He just stood there looking. Not moving, not doing anything, just staring at what he thought was himself. He knew at that moment that Malaika wasn't the only one to pass away on that fateful day. He knew in his heart that he had just died too. The only difference, there was no one there to celebrate his life or mourn his death.

If only he had been the man of the family the way *they* wanted him to, he would have known what to do now. After what seemed like an eternity, his sisters' beautiful features began to clarify themselves. "And the truth shall reveal itself". Malaika had once said. He needed to talk to her. He needed more time to tell her that he loved her. One more time to just look at her' and tell her that he could not be the person that she was. He just wanted one more chance.

He began to wail again. He lost his strength as he once again stumbled over the person behind him. This time he backed into Macon Alexander, their elderly, and "always on the scene" neighbor. Thank God, he was not pushed back to face his deceased sister lying there in the silk ruffles.

She seemed to be smiling as if she had a secret that she wanted to tease him with before she told him. It was like old times. Malaika would hold on to some juicy tidbit of information to tease him. As always, she would tell it but not one minute before her brother would frown his face up and declare that he didn't care. With a smile on her face, she would finally tell him. It seemed like even now, she had that same smile that let him know that she would tell her secret. His heart ached. It literally broke to pieces as the reality hit him that not only would she not be telling him this secret, there would never be any secrets shared between them. His guardian angel was no longer there to protect him. His sobs became uncontrollable as each thought crossed his mind. It was more than his heart could handle. It was more than he had ever had to deal with without Malaika and he didn't want to handle it. That was it. He just didn't want to. Malik was seated next to Lavina, who had finally come to. She made a sobbing noise that was barely audible.

The three remaining Scott's sat together on the first pew missing Malaika for their own personal reasons. Their minds raced in a gazillion different directions as the processions continued in front of them. There were children and adults all touched by the death of this angel. Several hands touched and patted each of them. There were women who would hug them and kiss them or press tissues and hankies into their hands as they brushed by. They were all either friends and or family members. They just wanted to help ease the pain. While they were trying to show their support, they would not allow eye contact. It was as if by eye contact, the pain would be contagious or transferable. The services were short and quaint. It would have been too much for the immediate family to have a long drawn out going home service.

One of Malaika's class mates sang *His Eye is on the Sparrow* and another sang Tamela Mann's *Take Me to the King*. Someone else read an original poem about being gone too soon. Pastor Burgess did the eulogy. His voice was deep but very smoothing.

"Our Father has come to call home one of his children," he said in an almost hypnotic song-speak. He spoke of the hope of a tree, "As it is cut down, there is hope that with the rain it will bud. *As the waters fail from the sea, and the flood decayeth and dryeth up: So man dieth down and riseth not.*"

He rested, panning the congregation with his eyes. His glaze fell on Lavina. He walked to her and placed his hand on her shoulder. She was still sobbing. Startled at the weight on her shoulder, she jumped but the lament never stopped and Pastor Burgess never stopped talking.

"Till the heavens be no more, they shall not awake nor be raised out of their sleep. The Lord has a job for this little sister." He paused, "though she may not be here in flesh, I want y'all to know that she's here in spirit." He patted each of them, resting his hand on each of their shoulders. He continued to speak to the congregation. He reminded them

of Christian Discipleship. Reminding them that this family would need them to pray for them and visit them periodically. These were His Sheep and members of this very flock. These are our brothers and sisters. Saints, we ought to remember what thus saith the Lord and live our lives and govern ourselves accordingly." In one singular motion, his large frame was back in the pulpit. Turning to them again, he called for the pall bearers as the choir began to sing *I'll Fly Away*.

The burial services were just as quick. There was prayer and dedication, scripture, and a song. All was brought to an end as Pastor Burgess finalized the ceremonies.

"I am the resurrection, and the life: he that believeth in me, though he were dead, yet shall he live: and whosoever liveth and believeth in me shall never die." He hugged and kissed the family again. He touched them gently and told them that he would be there for them when they needed.

"Saints, please know that my Father is a loving Father. You may not understand the whys and the intricacies of his decisions but it's not for us to know. Surrender to His will. Have faith; keep praying for direction and strength. My Father will answer your prayers." He was trying to direct each statement to the person that he felt would be most comforted by it. Knowing fully that each person heard it as they wanted and discarded whatever they could not use for their own personal benefit. He walked slowly back to the church hall where the repast for immediate family, close relatives and friends would be served. Pastor Burgess left each of them there with their own thoughts.

They missed her. They were standing there together as if they were all alone; sobbing, crying, and confused. Mechanically, they stood there waiting for Malaika to tell them what to do next. Who would take care of them? Who would make them smile? Who would bring peace? Who would brighten their days? Who would love them unconditionally, even when they felt they didn't deserve it?

"Why Lord?" they each asked. "Why?"

ABOUT THE AUTHOR

Winde! Washington-Nnochirionye was born in Pontiac, Michigan and is the third daughter of Randi Massey (Rock Hill, SC), the late William Howard Taft Washington, Jr., and the late Lonnie "Pops" Massey, Sr. Winde! has two older sisters and three younger brothers (one deceased). She is the proud mother of a pre-teen who is a promising poet, writer, and musician.

Winde! attended Bennett High School in Buffalo, New York. In her Senior year, she was an exchange student to Padua, Italy where she attended and graduated from high school at Alvise Cornaro Scuola Scientifico, an Italian speaking school. After high school, she attended Tuskegee University in Tuskegee, Alabama.

As a young world traveler, Winde! continued to travel throughout the country and abroad. She has lived in 9 different states and on 3 different continents. She lived and worked in Lagos, Nigeria for 3 years.

Winde! is a full time Train Dispatcher for the Norfolk Southern Railroad Corporation in Harrisburg, Pennsylvania. She is also the Sole Proprietor of Y.A.M.S. (Yet Another Mustard Seed) Creation©. Winde! uses her gifts and talent to enlighten, encourage, and teach those that she encounters. She writes poetry, fiction, short stories, blogs and performs spoken word. She is a motivational speaker and enjoys organizing and conducting seminars, workshops, and retreats for different groups. Winde! is currently in the publishing stages of her debut novel, *The Tempest Is Raging.*

A member of International Free and Accepted Modern Masons and Order of the Eastern Star, Inc., she considers herself a community advocate and activist and volunteers in many community service activities. She is also a lifetime Girl Scout.

Her favorite thing to do is write. Whether poetry, fiction, or speeches, her charge is to write the vision and make it plain. If she reaches one person, touches one person, or makes a difference in just one life, she feels her efforts will not have been in vain.